STARTING ANEW AFTER SEVENTY

*Dr. Podolco,
Just a token of appreciation for the fine message. Best wishes for continued success!*

Starting Anew After Seventy

The Story of
Ida Ella Jones, Primitive Artist

By
Ida J. Williams

J Williams
6-23-85

Illustrated

Exposition Press   *Hicksville, New York*

FIRST EDITION

© 1980 by Ida J. Williams

All rights reserved. No part of this book may be reproduced, in whole or in part, in any form or by any means, electronic or mechanical, including photocopying, recording, or by any information storage and retrieval system, without permission in writing from the publisher. Address inquiries to Exposition Press, Inc., 900 South Oyster Bay Road, Hicksville, NY 11801.

Library of Congress Catalog Card Number: 79-56925

ISBN 0-682-49544-1

Printed in the United States of America

To Mrs. Walter P. Townsend,
Mother's loyal and devoted friend

Contents

PREFACE ... ix

1. Life Anew ... 1
2. Productive Leisure Moments ... 3
3. Professor Bond's Visit ... 7
4. Mom's First One-Man Exhibition ... 10
5. Merits of a Hobby ... 14
6. Mom's Second One-Man Exhibition ... 17
7. Age Has No Barriers ... 19
8. Her Creations ... 23
9. Commendations and Recognitions ... 32
10. Ebb Tide ... 35
11. Posthumous Exhibits ... 37
12. Biographical Highlights ... 40

Preface

This book is based on major incidents in the life of my mother, Ida Ella Jones, from the age of seventy until her demise.

It is written with a fourfold purpose in mind: to relate the achievements of a latent talent developed into an exciting and rewarding career after age seventy; to show that one's productive years need not end with retirement, widowhood, or the withdrawal of children from the home; to inspire others to use the mature years for discovery, achievement, challenge, contentment, and fulfillment; to have a permanent record for family members, friends, and interested persons.

STARTING ANEW AFTER SEVENTY

1

Life Anew

Ida Ella Jones got out her sketchbook from the battered antique trunk to bring to life a latent talent, one that had been put aside for over a half century.

She was the wife of William Oscar Jones—pastor of the Church of Christ and retired blacksmith in the village of Ercildoun, Pennsylvania—and mother of twelve.

The enchanting field of artistic expression had fascinated her as far back as her eighth birthday when she was given a drawing book by her parents, Samuel and Louisa Ruth, and it was not long before her exceptional ability to draw lifelike fruits, vegetables, flowers, and birds was recognized by her parents, grade school teacher, and Mrs. Lucretia Haines for whom she worked back in the 1890s.

In 1892, Mrs. Haines saw some of her drawings and commended her for the fine work that she had done. She offered to give her free painting lessons if she would buy her own materials. Mom, thrilled with the idea, agreed to the plan.

Three lessons in the use of oil paints and the supervision of one complete canvas, *The Fisherman*, followed. A second painting, *Moonlight on the Lake*, was partially finished when she accepted a proposal for marriage.

Amidst the hustle and bustle of preparations for her wedding, she put away her sketchbook and palette, with the idea that at some future date she would resume her favorite hobby.

Now past seventy, when many persons have considered their creative years passed, she has returned to the field of art and has found it rewarding and fulfilling.

The setting was right for the resumption of a lifelong interest. Previously, there had been few leisure moments as she catered to family needs, helped her husband—better known as Pop—with his ministerial duties and blacksmithing trade.

But it was not only family and wifely duties that kept her occupied. Her pleasant disposition, kind deeds, hospitality to community members and friends—regardless of race, color, or creed—earned her the appellation Mom to many.

Now, there was no need to make double recipes of bread, pack seven lunch boxes, can hundreds of jars of fruits and vegetables, wash two or three times a week, and nurse the ailing back to health.

Ten of the twelve children had been reared and were now married or pursuing their own careers. The nest was empty.

Moreover, a chronic physical condition required restful hours and fewer of the many household chores. Empty moments began to be extremely boring. As Mom sat thinking of what to do with her spare time, she remarked aloud:

"I wonder if I can still paint?"

Her daughter-in-law, the late Carol Brodus Jones, who dropped in for a brief visit as she was meditating over the possibility of trying her hand at painting, was sent for a few art supplies, with Mom anxiously awaiting her return. While she waited, she reminisced about the past as she looked through the old faded sketchbook and selected subjects for try-outs.

Her work began with small projects—flowers, birds, fruits, and simple landscapes. Each was painted from her own experience and the world around her.

The results pleased her.

Family members and friends, amazed at the great display of talent, all wanted to know when and how it all began.

2

Productive Leisure Moments

The techniques for working with oil paints came back to her as she recalled those first few lessons with Mrs. Haines over fifty years before. When her grandson, Owen Leon Jones, Jr. (Teddy), who was in elementary school, stopped by for a visit with his watercolor set that had been used at school, Mom asked him to give her a demonstration of its use. This pleased Teddy immensely, and she was so happy with the results that she sent for a set for herself. Consequently, her work included both oil and watercolor projects.

The joy and satisfaction she derived from artistic expression could be seen in her elation, as she hurried to complete other chores in order to get back to her palette.

Encouraged by family and friends to develop this hobby that had been hidden for such a long time, she sketched interesting and challenging scenes, scrutinizing the environment for subjects then returning to her easel to complete the composition.

Almost any occasion could prompt an inspiration to paint, such as the time my husband, Charles, and I were visiting her for a holiday from our home in Eastern Shore, Virginia, and had brought along Bubbles, our cocker spaniel.

We were busy chatting over events when we heard Bubbles

had the special job of painting and repairing picture frames contributed by his nephew Roland Johnson, who secured them at sales and auctions.

An invitation to become a member and participate in the exhibits of the local Chester County Art Association broadened Mom's horizons. Many more people had an opportunity to see her work. Art critics praised her achievements.

2

Productive Leisure Moments

The techniques for working with oil paints came back to her as she recalled those first few lessons with Mrs. Haines over fifty years before. When her grandson, Owen Leon Jones, Jr. (Teddy), who was in elementary school, stopped by for a visit with his watercolor set that had been used at school, Mom asked him to give her a demonstration of its use. This pleased Teddy immensely, and she was so happy with the results that she sent for a set for herself. Consequently, her work included both oil and watercolor projects.

The joy and satisfaction she derived from artistic expression could be seen in her elation, as she hurried to complete other chores in order to get back to her palette.

Encouraged by family and friends to develop this hobby that had been hidden for such a long time, she sketched interesting and challenging scenes, scrutinizing the environment for subjects then returning to her easel to complete the composition.

Almost any occasion could prompt an inspiration to paint, such as the time my husband, Charles, and I were visiting her for a holiday from our home in Eastern Shore, Virginia, and had brought along Bubbles, our cocker spaniel.

We were busy chatting over events when we heard Bubbles

barking furiously. We all rushed to the window, only to see Mom's house cat seated comfortably on a limb of the old maple tree in the front yard, with Bubbles at the base of the trunk daring him to come down.

This incident was the inspiration for the painting *Bubbles Don't Like Cats*.

On another occasion, Mom and Pop rode with her brother, William Chester Ruth, to visit friends in West Virginia. As they left the populated area and got out into the hills, mountains, and sites of the oil wells, she was impressed by the picturesque countryside and sketched several scenes as they motored through the territory. The paintings produced from this trip were *West Virginia Oil Wells*, *The Hurst Home, West Virginia*, and *Near Bristol*.

During the spring of 1946 Mom and Pop visited us in Virginia. The woods and yards were spotted with blooming dogwood. Other spring shrubs and flowers were bursting forth in their splendor, offering numerous ideas for the artist's canvas.

Pop brought in a couple of branches of white dogwood and Mom went to work in her sketchbook. The final canvas—a 21½" × 23" oil—is *Virginia's Dogwood*.

During their stay in Virginia, we spent a number of afternoons driving through the country and down by the Chesapeake Bay in Cape Charles. We parked at a point on the busy Cape Charles waterfront where Mom could see the triple-decked ferry, the honking tugboats, and the numerous fishermen, come and go. It was interesting to watch the docking activities and observe the cars and hilarious passengers as they traveled to and fro.

The water, sunset, and boating activities were stimuli for creativity. It was gratifying to see the enthusiasm and zeal with which Mom painted *Passenger Boat*, *Leaving Cape Charles*, *Tugboat*, and *Cape Charles, Virginia*. Each moment was precious and each project very special.

One of the crops raised on our small twenty-acre farm in Pennsylvania was strawberries. Each June the family members would be up at the break of day and out amidst the morning

Productive Leisure Moments

dew picking the ripened berries so as to make the early market and fill the orders for the fruit.

Mom's interest in strawberries can be seen in a number of paintings in which they were subjects. She had a unique way of making the seeds in the berries look natural. When questioned about her technique, she would always give a little chuckle and say, "That's my little secret."

Some inspirations for canvases went back to experiences during the early days of marriage, such as *Horse and Buggy Days*.

It was the time Mom and Pop had shopped carefully for each item on the memorandum, placed them in the back of their secondhand buggy, and headed for home. They talked about their bargains and hummed together familiar old tunes as Jack, their favorite horse, trotted down the dusty country road. It was not until they arrived home that they discovered that the old buggy had lost part of its bottom and their groceries.

Lack of formal training did not thwart her efforts to express her love for plants, animals, flowers, fruits, people through her oils and watercolors, as she portrayed her own experiences in the world in which she lived. Soon Mom began to be recognized as an exceptionally good primitive artist.

Many of the first small paintings were given as gifts to family members in the area and to friends who visited. In spite of this, the walls of the modest living room began to be covered with them.

The idea of selling some of her productions came to her. She talked it over with Pop and they agreed that income from the sales would supplement the family's cash and make room for other creations. Pop constructed a rustic billboard from secondhand lumber on which Mom printed the words—ART WORK FOR SALE. It was placed at the end of the road alongside the mailbox. A smaller sign was made and nailed to the old maple tree in front of the homestead.

Curious and interested persons were attracted by the signs, and the market for her paintings began to grow. Both Mom and Pop were kept busy entertaining customers and filling orders. Pop had the special job of painting and repairing picture frames contributed by his nephew Roland Johnson, who secured them at sales and auctions.

An invitation to become a member and participate in the exhibits of the local Chester County Art Association broadened Mom's horizons. Many more people had an opportunity to see her work. Art critics praised her achievements.

3

Professor Bond's Visit

It was a beautiful spring morning. Mom awakened early from habit rather than from necessity. She dressed quickly, putting on a favorite gingham apron; then she carried out a few early morning chores and ate a light breakfast.

She had become widowed in April 1947, just a short time after she had revived her interest in artistic expression. Although Pop's death had come as a shock to all the family, Mom was doing an outstanding job in adjusting to the loss. More and more of her time was devoted to her blooming career, evident in the increased number of pieces of work produced.

That morning she had gone to her easel and was pondering over the finishing touches for a landscape when the silence was broken by approaching footsteps. As they crossed the old wooden porch that joined the hundred-year log cabin to the main structure of the house, she paused, turning her thin, slightly bent body, and listened as they grew closer.

The sound of several rapid knocks confirmed her suspicions that she was about to have a visitor. Putting down her paint brush, she got up and pushed back a wisp of gray hair that had escaped from the taut bun and moved slowly toward the door.

"Yes! Yes! One moment, please."

A quick look through the sheer tailored curtains revealed the figure of a tall, stately, brown-skinned man. As she opened the door he removed his hat and bowed politely.

"How do you do, Mrs. Jones. I am Horace M. Bond, president of Lincoln University. I'm doing some research on the Underground Railroad. A house in this area was used as one of the stations. A neighbor directed me to you for information concerning it."

"Oh, yes! Please come in, Mr. Bond."

Professor Bond, historian and president of Lincoln University, Chester County's oldest institution for higher learning, was extremely active in civic affairs. One of his projects involved research on the route of the Underground Railroad that was so active in helping slaves escape to freedom during the time before the Civil War.

As Professor Bond stepped inside the humble living room, his eyes caught the array of oil and watercolor paintings of all sizes and in every available space. For a moment he was silent as he looked from one to the other.

"Who is responsible for all this?" he asked.

"Why, why, I am," Mom replied as she blushed slightly.

"I haven't heard anything about you. Have you exhibited your work?" he asked as he walked from one painting to another.

"Yes, I've shown some of my work in the annual shows of the Chester County Art Association. Their exhibits are held in the Coatesville, Downingtown, and West Chester areas. The towns are just a few miles from here. I've gained a number of friends and admirers as a result."

"Where did you receive your training, Mrs. Jones?"

"There were just a few lessons from Mrs. Haines in 1892 prior to my marriage. Tips on the use of watercolors came from my grandson."

Mom walked over to the sofa and pointed out the oil painting *The Fisherman,* which hung above.

"This is the one on which I received lessons over fifty years ago."

"Why such a long delay in the development of so much talent?"

"I was the third daughter in a family of ten children. We lived on a farm which kept everyone busy. During the fall and winter months, my older sisters and I worked for families in the community to help increase the family income. So there was little time or money for me to pursue my interest in art. Then, I met a fine young man who proposed marriage. We raised ten children. I had to put away my paintings with the hope that at some future date I would return to my favorite hobby."

Professor Bond was silent as he studied the landscape that had been completed over fifty years ago. It had tall evergreen trees and mountainous peaks in the background; a clouded sky hovered over a lone fisherman seated on a rugged rock with his fishing line dangling in the rough stream below.

"Others must meet you and see this marvelous work," he said. "Lincoln University will present you in a one-man exhibition of paintings."

"Oh, thank you! Thank you! It will be an honor to exhibit my work at the university."

They finally got around to discussing the Underground Railroad. The house involved was on the neighboring farm and had been owned by Mom's parents.

The visit proved to be rewarding to both parties. Professor Bond got information for his research project and he also discovered a humble rural artist. He left her elated over the prospect of her first one-man exhibition of paintings.

4

Mom's First One-Man Exhibition

The walls of Vail Memorial Library at Lincoln University were hung with selected oils and watercolors of the elderly primitive artist from the small village of Ercildoun on November 15, 1951. It was the opening of Mom's first one-man exhibition.

There was a constant flow of university personnel, professional artists, art lovers, curious onlookers, friends, and relatives. They had come to see and evaluate the work of the newly acclaimed artist.

Mom, neatly attired in her black dress with white collar and matching accessories, sat at the head of the reception table as a hostess poured tea.

Her eyes brightened as a warm pleasant smile deepened the graceful lines that spread across her forehead and cheeks. She bowed her head humbly as she extended her hand to the many visitors, chatting and answering questions about various paintings and her long delay in returning to the fascinating world of art.

Her sincere delight in her latent talent in bloom showed in her flushed face and in the zeal with which she reminisced with the guests and friends over the inspiration that prompted her return to the easel.

Mom's First One-Man Exhibition

The Committee on Exhibitions for Lincoln University wrote the following in its brochure:

> Her work recalls that of Henri Rousseau and Horace Pippin, but she is creative and fully deserves consideration and respect for her achievements.
> She has illustrative character in common with early American black silhouette cut-outs on white paper or the Pennsylvania Dutch highly decorative ornamental patterns of birds and tulips. Her color is mostly in bright luminous areas which give the appearance of being solid but are internally mottled by brush-work as a means of giving the delicacy which she seeks to express. It is a major factor in telling her story or carrying out her decorative floral patterns. Although she may be termed a primitive artist, it does not mean that her expression is without parallel in the traditions of art.

The *Coatesville Record*, a local newspaper, had this to say relative to the one-man exhibition:

> Since her first drawing some sixty-eight years ago, Mrs. Jones has done the unbelievable, by producing paintings that have astounded the experts.

During the course of this eventful occasion, Mom told some of the incidents that had served as an inspiration for a particular work.

The *Haunted House*, for example, was inspired by the events that happened during her early years of marriage.

In their search for good housing accommodations, Mom and Pop decided to ignore all tales and rent an average looking three-bedroom house in the rural area of Stottsville, Pennsylvania, that had the reputation of being haunted. All went well for a while. Then they began to see lighted areas at random intervals on the grounds. Then once, in the middle of the night, Haines, their five-year-old son, awakened them yelling, "Get out of here! Get out of here!"

They rushed into his room to see whatever was causing the disturbance. Nothing could be seen, but Haines kept pointing at something at the foot of his bed. Eventually they got him quiet and returned to their own room, puzzled. This incident was repeated frequently.

The climax came when Mom and her sister Elizabeth Johnson were spending the afternoon chatting and sewing in the living room. Suddenly, they both heard something like screams in the chimney and fireplace area.

Mom rushed upstairs to get the baby, who was taking his afternoon nap. When she returned, the screams had ceased, leaving two frightened women pale and speechless.

That settled it. The next day Mom and Pop went house hunting.

As the professionals in the field of art moved from one canvas to another, they saw her vision of the natural world as experienced in her lifestyle.

Horse and Buggy Days, Oil Wells of West Virginia, The Cape Charles Boat were among the many wonderful works that greatly impressed the experts when they learned the age and background of the artist.

The one-man exhibition was the beginning of the fulfillment of a childhood dream that added new dimensions and purpose for living. It was an exciting and uplifting experience that opened the door for continued self expression, involvement, constructive use of leisure, and financial rewards.

And this new way of life began after seventy.

* * *

The following works were exhibited from November 12, 1951, to December 14, 1951, in the Vail Memorial Library:

OILS

1. Horse and Buggy Days
2. French Landscape
3. Mums
4. Early Winter
5. Dogwood
6. Oil Wells of West Virginia
7. Cape Charles Boat
8. Dionne Quintuplets
9. Light Snow

10. COLD WAVE
11. A LOAD OF LIVESTALK (sic)
12. PARABLE OF THE TEN VIRGINS
13. AUTUMN FLOWERS
14. PETUNIAS
15. HAUNTED HOUSE
16. BEST MILKER

WATERCOLORS

17. DISH OF FRUIT
18. STRAWBERRIES AND GRAPES
19. OWEN ON HIS HORSE
20. SHOEING A HORSE

5

Merits of a Hobby

One's interest and enthusiasm toward purposeful living regardless of age are in direct proportion to his or her joys, satisfactions, and healthy outlook.

Though widowed and ofttimes alone, Mom found her hobby to be a tremendous asset. She concentrated on the beautiful world in which she lived, and became more involved with creative expression. The meticulous manner in which she planned and worked on each painting evidenced her love for the work; her ability for expression was a precious gift.

Her chain of friends and customers increased as a result of the exhibition at Lincoln University. Among them were Mr. and Mrs. Walter P. Townsend of Cheyney, Pennsylvania, who, also, sponsored an exhibition of her work in their home on February 17, 1952.

Mrs. Townsend became widowed some time after the exhibition. She, too, had additional spare moments that could be filled. As an admirer of Mom's work and a connoisseur of the arts, she was the one who made the contacts and transported Mom to a number of the art centers and galleries where she received recognition.

Merits of a Hobby

The two used leisure moments of some of the lovely spring and fall days to drive through the country in search of unique scenes for the canvas. Her desk became cluttered with little sketches of scenes captured as she rode through the countryside, as well as with visions of the past and those odd subjects encountered in her everyday life. Each had its own setting and her individual interpretation.

Visitors and buyers spent many pleasant moments with Mom at home as she explained the background for various subjects developed in her creations.

On one occasion, she picked up the painting titled *The Cherry Tree Robbery*.

"Every morning I used to watch the blackbirds stealing my fruit from that tree over there on the hill. We never had many cherries left for the family and it used to make me so unhappy. So, you see, I've at least caught the robbers in the act," she said as she returned it to the easel.

As the living room walls lost a number of their pictures to sales, new paintings took their place. There was that constant urge to create.

From her biblical training and experience as a minister's wife she was influenced to portray a scene found in Matthew 25:1-14, *The Parable of the Ten Virgins*. This oil has been a favorite to many and was selected to illustrate the announcement of an exhibition of her works in March 1978 at the Chester County Art Association gallery.

The painting, a night scene, depicts the five wise virgins carrying their burning lamps as they go to greet the bridegroom; the five foolish virgins are on their way to the merchant to buy oil for their lamps as a full moon shines overhead.

Affiliation with the Chester County Art Association enriched her experiences, increased her clientele, and drew attention to her work, because she was often the oldest exhibitor in the show.

The little homemade billboard at the end of the road continued to draw friends and customers. Reporters came for interviews, and articles concerning her achievements appeared in such newspapers as the *Coatesville Record,* West Chester's *Daily Local News,* and the *Philadelphia Tribune.*

Her work was exhibited in schools, private homes, stores, the West Chester Courthouse lawn, clubs and galleries in the Philadelphia area—Everyman's Gallery, The Little Gallery, The Pyramid Club—and by a collector in New York City.

Visitors from California, West Virginia, New York, Connecticut, Delaware, Maryland, New Jersey, and Virginia came to meet the artist and, often, to buy her paintings. Mom was beginning to reap financial rewards. Her hobby had became a challenging career that filled every spare moment.

6

Mom's Second One-Man Exhibition

Scenes of the awakening spring, blooming flowers, colorful fall foliage, of people, pets, and events in her life continued to serve as inspiration for her many unique and varied oil and watercolor paintings, revealing the personality, experiences, and world of this newly acclaimed primitive artist.

On February 17, 1952, her friends Mr. and Mrs. Walter P. Townsend of Cheyney, Pennsylvania, art lovers and admirers of her work, sponsored a one-man exhibition in their home.

The late Mr. Townsend was the director of the Pennsylvania Children's Aid Society; Mrs. Townsend was active in art circles and civic and community projects. Their sincere interest and respect for Mom and her achievements prompted them to honor her with this showing of her work.

The thought of it all pleased Mom immensely. She was extremely grateful for the privilege to meet and share information concerning her work with others.

For the showing, twenty-eight oils and watercolors were selected and hung throughout the beautiful colonial home of Mr. and Mrs. Townsend.

The president of Cheyney College, faculty members, artists,

and friends were given the privilege of viewing the works of this elderly artist who had just enjoyed her seventy-eighth birthday.

The following paintings were included in the exhibit:

OILS

1. A LOAD OF LIVESTALK (sic)
2. BIRTHDAY FLOWERS
3. CAPE CHARLES, VIRGINIA
4. DEER SEASON
5. HORSE AND BUGGY DAYS
6. MY DAFFODILS
7. PASTURE SEASON
8. THE PARABLE OF THE TEN VIRGINS
9. TUGBOAT, CAPE CHARLES, VIRGINIA
10. WEST VIRGINIA OIL WELLS #2
11. WE TRAVELED THIS WAY IN 1892

WATERCOLORS

12. DISH OF FRUIT
13. JONES HOME
14. MOCK ORANGE
15. OLD TOM, OUR HOUSE CAT #1
16. PHLOX
17. STRAWBERRIES AND GRAPES #2
18. THE GAME WARDEN'S HOME
19. WEDDING CAKE HOUSE

UNFRAMED OILS

20. BIRDS LIKE CHERRIES
21. DISH OF STRAWBERRIES

UNFRAMED WATERCOLORS

22. GERANIUM FLOWERS
23. MY FATHER'S HOME, 1880, SAMUEL RUTH
24. OLD TOM, OUR HOUSE CAT #2
25. STRAWBERRIES AND GRAPES #1
26. STRAWBERRIES AND GRAPES #3
27. WEDDING CAKE HOUSE #2
28. ZINNIAS

7

Age Has No Barriers

Mom's work was considered by art critics as unique and worthy of recognition, despite her age. Invitations continued to come from individuals, organizations, and special groups for a display of her work. She was often the oldest exhibitor in the shows sponsored by clubs and galleries.

Rather than a handicap, her advanced age was a stimulus to make the best use of available opportunities, to develop her potential to the highest, and to fill her newly acquired leisure with constructive and enjoyable experiences.

Notes from her itinerary indicate her busy schedule.

Fall of 1948: Nineteen of her paintings were shown on the West Chester Courthouse lawn as a part of the annual Clothesline Show of the members of the Chester County Art Association.

October 17, 1949: Pennsylvania Week—The following paintings were exhibited in Speakman's Bookstore, Coatesville, Pennsylvania:

1. MORNING GLORY (oil)
2. THE FISHERMAN (oil)
3. QUINTS EATING WATERMELON (watercolor)

October 19, 1949: Exhibit at Everyman's Art Gallery, Philadelphia:

OILS

1. COLD WAVE
2. FISHING IN 1892
3. MOCK ORANGE
4. STRAWBERRIES

WATERCOLORS

5. LANCASTER HIGHWAY
6. MY OWN HOME

October 1950: Pennsylvania Week—Exhibit in Speakman's Bookstore:

OILS

1. COLD WAVE
2. OIL FIELDS OF WEST VIRGINIA
3. OIL WELLS
4. OLD TOM
5. OX TEAM
6. MOONLIGHT ON THE LAKE
7. MUMS
8. ROSES

April 29, 1950: Exhibit at Chester County Art Show, West Chester:

OILS

1. VIRGINIA'S DOGWOOD
2. HORSE AND BUGGY DAYS (Received honorable mention)
3. MUMS
4. STRAWBERRIES

In March 1952, at age seventy-seven, she was the oldest of 115 artists who exhibited at the Pyramid Club Art Show in Philadelphia, Pennsylvania.

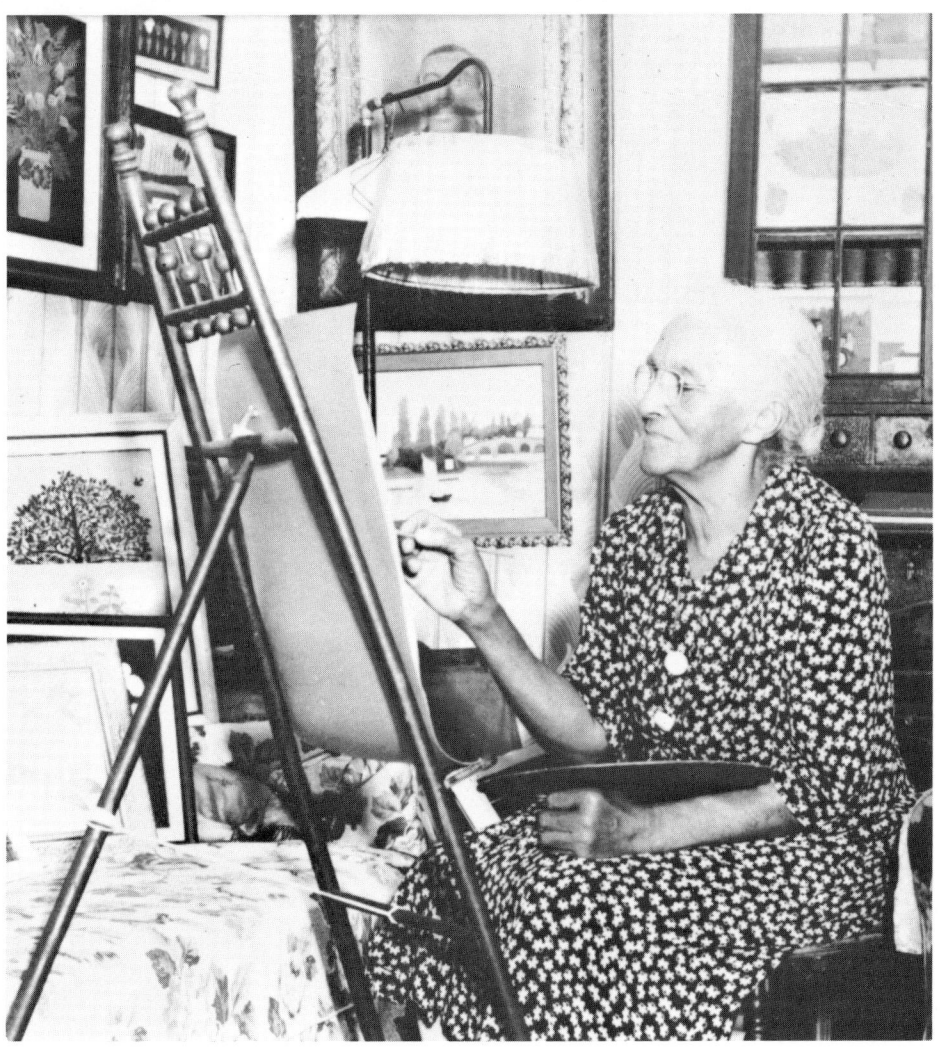
The artist at work. Oil and watercolor paintings in all sizes fill every available space.

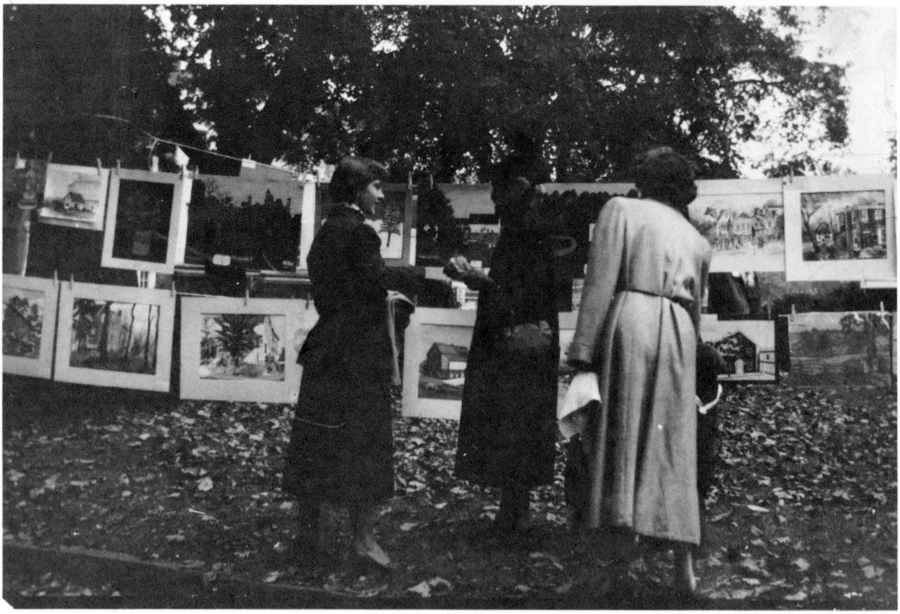

Mrs. Jones (center) discusses some of the people, places, and things that inspired her work, with two interested patrons of the Clothesline Show on the lawn of the West Chester, Pennsylvania, Courthouse, in 1948.

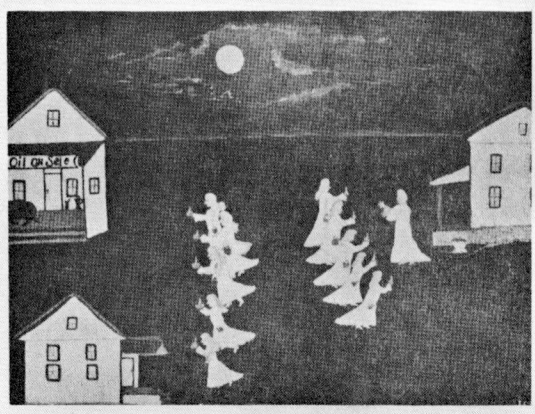

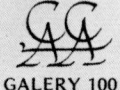

GALERY 100

IDA E. JONES

PENNSYLVANIA PRIMITIVE PAINTER
1874 - 1959

You are cordially invited to attend
the opening reception: Sun., Mar. 12, 1978

GALLERY HOURS
Sun. 3-5 p.m., Tues.-Sat. noon-4 p.m.

Exhibition continues through Mar. 26

The announcement of the Chester County Art Association in West Chester, showing her oil THE PARABLE OF THE TEN VIRGINS

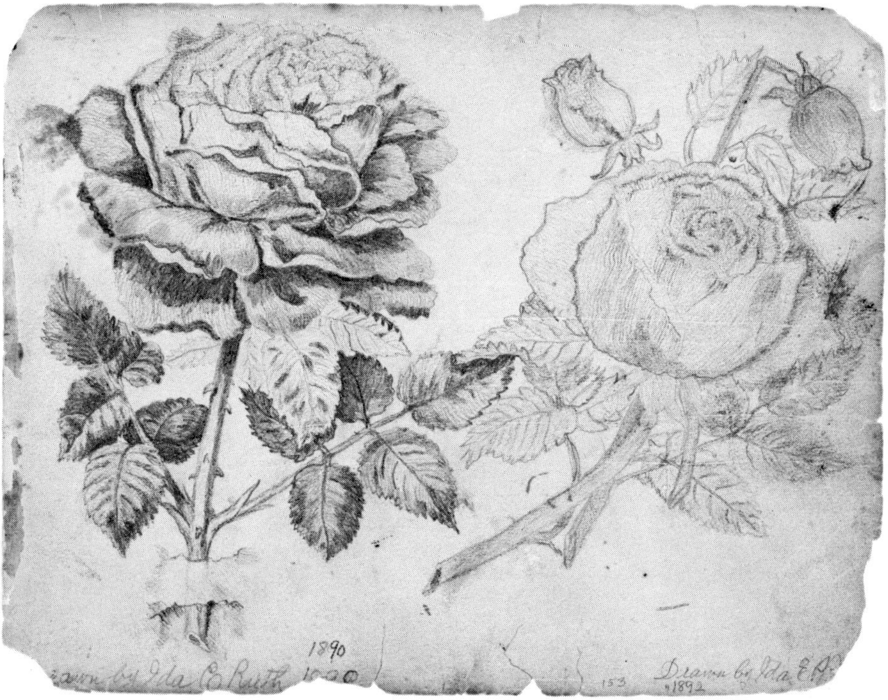

These penciled drawings are from the artist's original sketchbook. The roses were drawn in 1890, when she was sixteen, and the swan a year later.

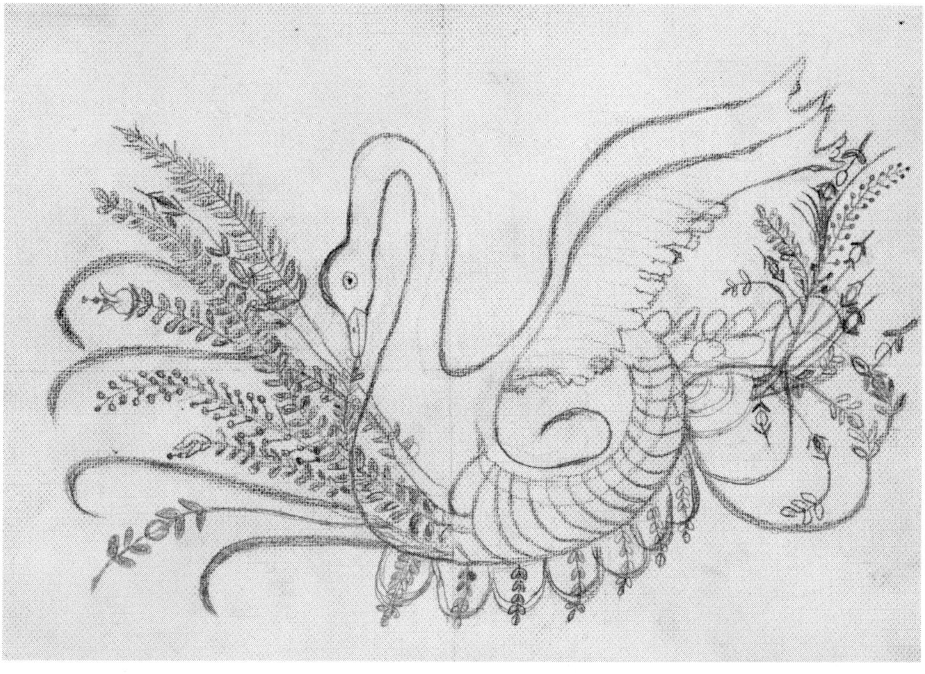

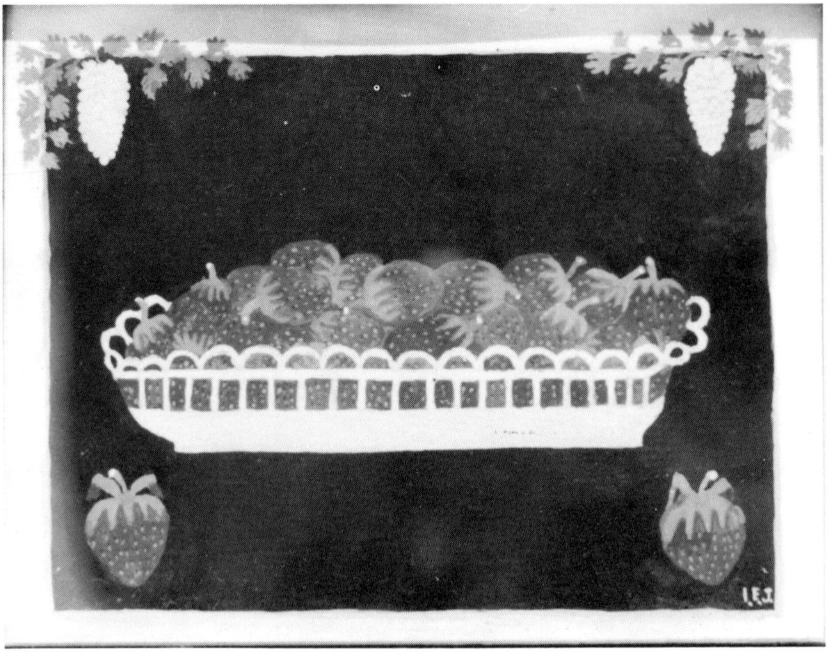

STRAWBERRIES (oil)

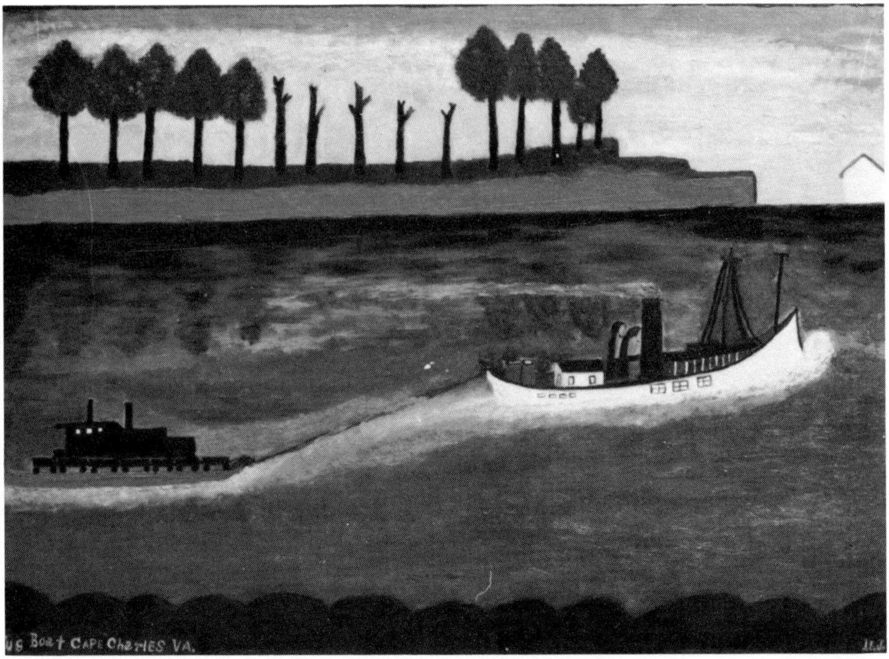

TUGBOAT (oil)

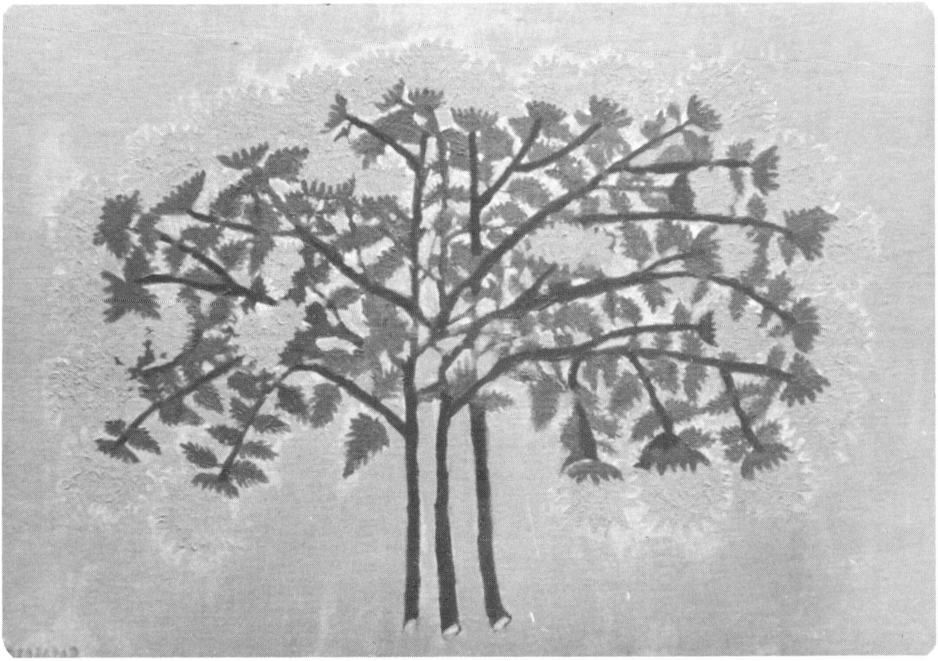

Pink Mums (oil)

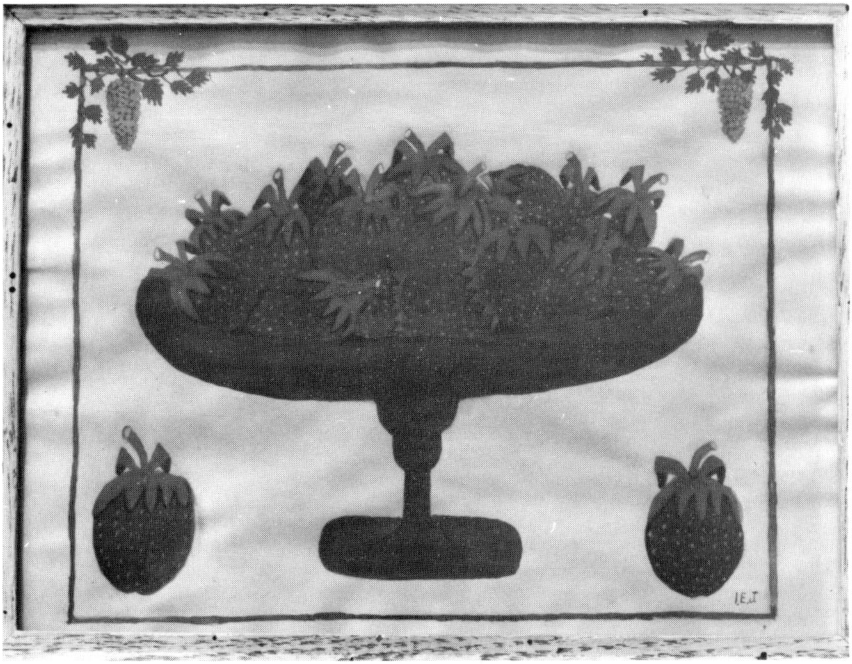

Strawberries and Grapes (watercolor)

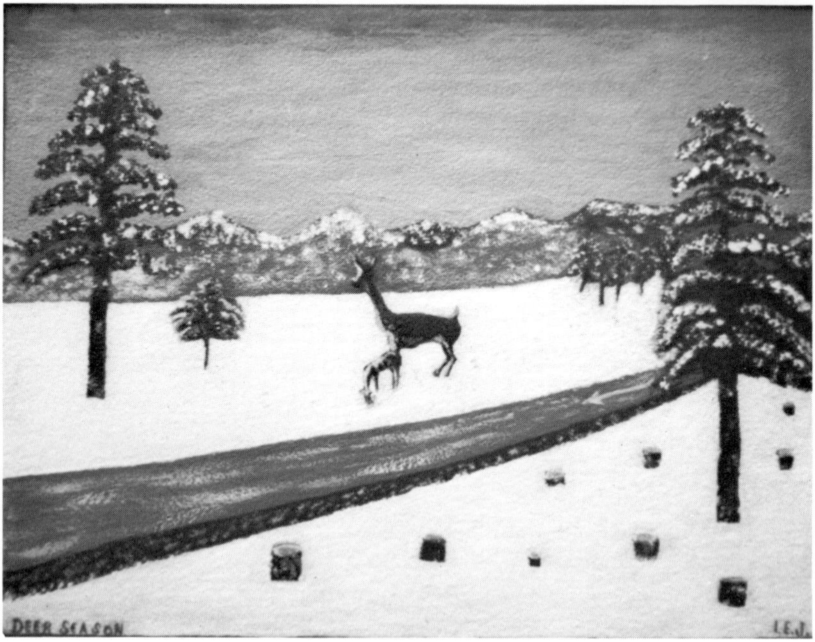

DEER SEASON (oil)

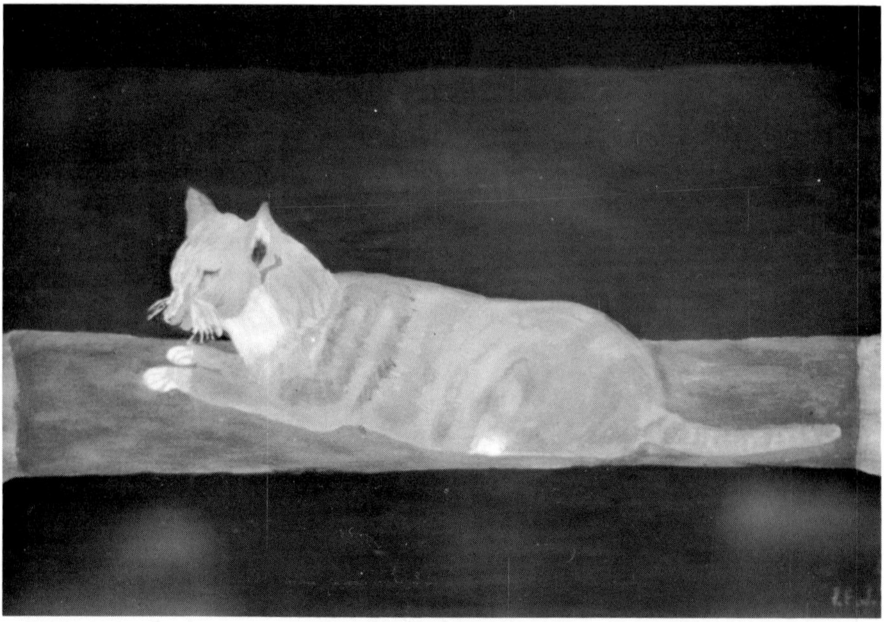

OLD TOM (watercolor)

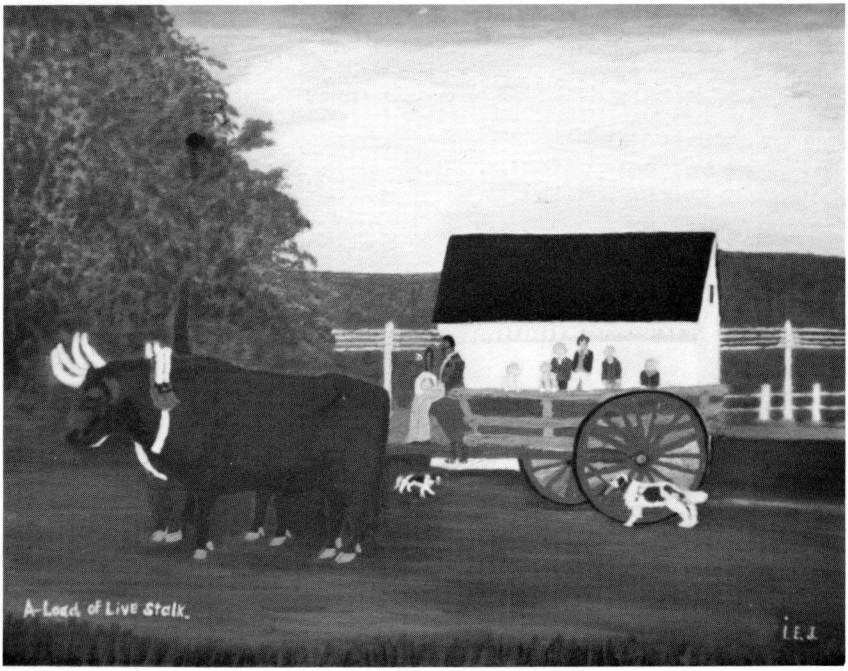

A LOAD OF LIVESTALK [sic] (oil)

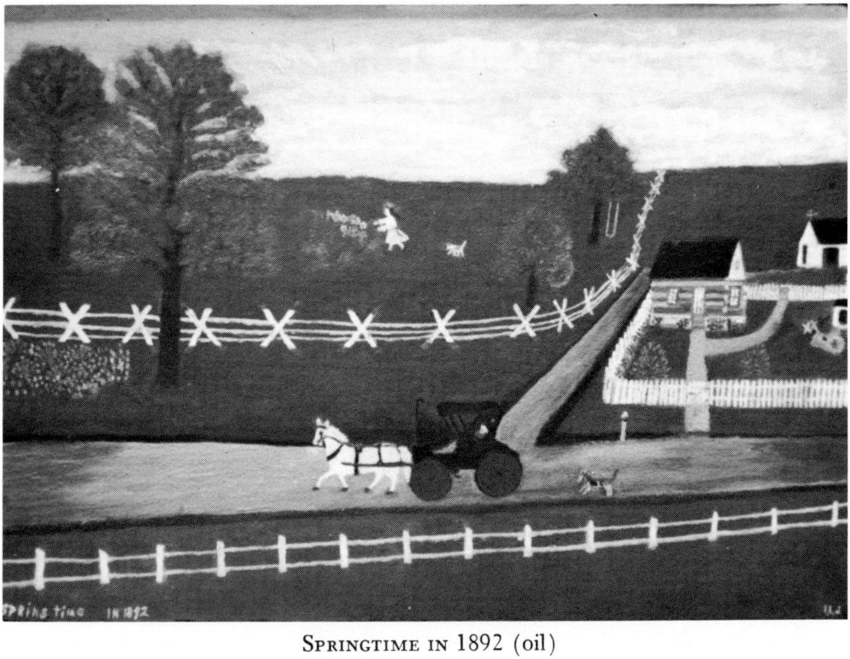

SPRINGTIME IN 1892 (oil)

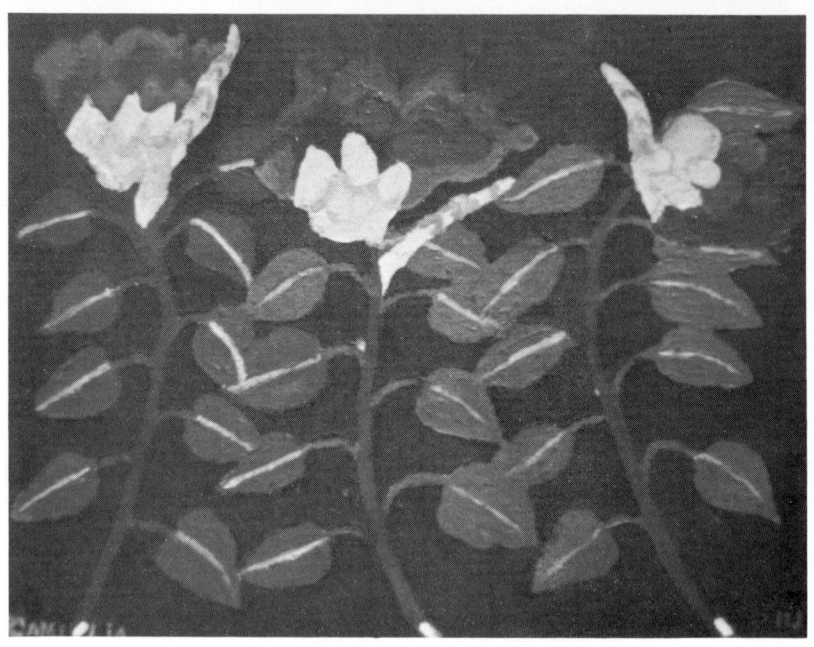

CAMELIAS (watercolor)

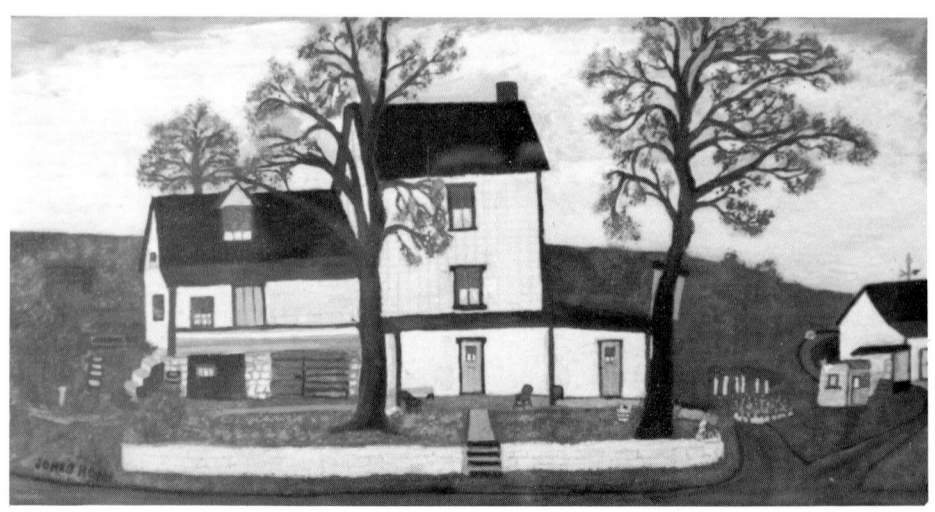

WILLIAM O. JONES HOMESTEAD (watercolor)

Age Has No Barriers

She was represented by her *Mums*, a striking oil of white chrysanthemums on long green stems, arranged fanshaped on a dull background. The painting caught the attention of a New York collector who later visited her home on April 27, 1952, and purchased seventeen others.

At seventy-nine, she continued to express herself through the medium of oil and watercolor paintings. It became her daily occupation.

Her work was given special recognition on the opening day of the Community Center Art Show in West Chester, Pennsylvania, in May 1953.

The oil painting *Moonlight on the Lake*, begun in 1893, had been completed and was on exhibit with several others.

A reporter asked, "Why was there such a long delay in its completion?"

She replied, "Well, ten children are a lot for any woman to help raise. Children and painting just didn't mix."

Her zeal for living a full and useful life kept her young and alert in mind in spite of the calendar years. She got into the act and responded stalwartly to life's challenges. Her work continued to earn recognition, as shown in the following excerpt from an article that appeared in the *Coatesville Record* in the spring of 1954:

Ercildoun Woman, at 80, Is Being Recognized as Outstanding Painter

A homemade sign, scarcely a foot wide, which is posted on a tree outside her home with the modest announcement, "Art Work for Sale," would hardly indicate to the passer-by that a talented artist lives inside.

Yet, the art work so modestly advertised by eighty-year-old Mrs. Ida E. Jones, of Ercildoun, who didn't take up painting until she was in her seventy-second year, is slowly winning more and more recognition among art circles in Philadelphia and New York.

Only recently, Mrs. Jones sold fifteen paintings to Allan Wolf, wealthy New York art collector, who came across her work in an Art Alliance exhibit in Philadelphia.

Intrigued with her primitive-style paintings, Wolf immediately made arrangements to come to Chester County to visit Mrs. Jones through a friend of his, Kenneth Stoner, a New York City landscape architect and a native of Sadsburyville.

Wolf, who frequently sponsors new and unknown artists in a similar fashion, is now planning to hold a one-man art exhibit of Mrs. Jones' painting sometime this fall. Already friends in New York, to whom he has shown her paintings, have expressed considerable interest in her work.

Mrs. Jones' paintings also have come to the attention of Fleur Cowles, co-publisher of *Look* magazine and other publications, who recently purchased a snow scene from the Ercildoun artist. . . .

8

Her Creations

The unusual manner in which Mom launched her art career made it difficult to get an accurate account of her paintings. There were at least three hundred pieces of work produced between the years 1945 and 1959.

No record was made of the many early works given to her children, grandchildren, and other relatives and friends.

The little homemade sign—ART WORK FOR SALE—drew customers who purchased many of her early pieces of work. Those who did not buy probably were given a souvenir of her intriguing, newly acclaimed hobby. The paintings, like her delicious gingercakes that were popular with all the children in the neighborhood, delighted the recipients and at the same time spread the news about her accomplishments.

In 1958 Mom helped my sister Lucy M. Searles and me to record the following works:

1945

OIL

1. A Gift from Isabel Stokes	13″	× 14″
2. Isabel and Ziba Stokes Residence	10″	× 16″
3. Route 50 West Virginia	18″	× 24″
4. Sunset in Virginia	10″	× 18″
5. Ruth Home in 1880	13″	× 14″
6. Phlox	16″	× 20″
7. Virginia's Dogwood	21″	× 23″
8. White Night	12″	× 16″

WATERCOLOR

9. Peacock	4¼″	× 5⅝″
10. The Bunting	4¼″	× 5⅝″
11. Bobby's Ride	4″	× 6″
12. My Sister's Home	10″	× 18″
13. Zinnias	4¼″	× 5⅝″
14. Daisies	4¼″	× 5⅝″
15. Route 50 West Virginia	18″	× 24″
16. My First in Thirty-Seven Years	12″	× 9″
17. Ruth Home—1930	10″	× 18″
18. Eclipse of Moon (set of 4)	3″	× 5″
19. The Beauties of Nature	27″	× 20″
20. Apple Blossoms	14″	× 18″

1946

OIL

21. Oil Well of West Virginia	18″	× 24″
22. The Hurst Home	15″	× 12″
23. Cape Charles, Virginia	12″	× 16″
24. West Virginia Oil Wells	18″	× 24″
25. Near Bristol, West Virginia	18″	× 24″

WATERCOLOR

26. Ercildoun Hall	10″	× 12″
27. Walter Holbrook Residence	10″	× 12″
28. Tugboat, Cape Charles, Virginia	10″	× 14″
29. Annual Meeting, 6/9/46	20″	× 25″
30. Sunset at Cape Charles	10″	× 18″
31. Phlox	16″	× 20″
32. Mountain Road	18″	× 24″
33. John F. Banks Residence, Virginia	14″	× 18″

1947

OIL

34. Our Old Chevrolet	8″	× 10″
35. Samuel Ruth's Threshing Rig, 1887	20″	× 30″
36. Church of Christ	4″	× 6″
37. Haunted House	11″	× 13″

WATERCOLOR

38. Homeplace	3″	× 5″
39. Harpers Ferry	18″	× 24″
40. The Bridge	14″	× 18″
41. Tulips	13″	× 15″
42. Ercildoun Hall	10″	× 12″

1948

OIL

43. Petunias	3″	× 4″
44. Cats Don't Like Dogs	8″	× 10″
45. Owen's Horses in Pasture	7″	× 9″
46. Blacksmith Shop	8″	× 10″
47. A Gift	18″	× 24″
48. Roses	16″	× 18″

WATERCOLOR

49. Dog in the Night	5″	× 6″
50. Nasturtium	5″	× 6″
51. Fruit	11″	× 14″
52. Fruit for Sale	11″	× 14″

1949

OIL

53. Above Lancaster	16″	× 20″
54. Birthday Roses	5″	× 3″
55. Dogwood	16″	× 21″

WATERCOLOR

56. Happy New Year	4″	× 5″
57. Eclipse of Moon (4 sections)	3″	× 5″
58. Owen Jones, Sr.	8″	× 10″

1950

OIL

59. Moonlight on the Lake	15″	× 20″
60. Cold Wave	16″	× 20″
61. Cold Wave	16″	× 21″
62. Mrs. Roosevelt and Her Great-grandson	6″	× 8″

WATERCOLOR

63. Ruth Home in 1930	13″	× 14″
64. Wedding Anniversary Card	4″	× 5″
65. Corsage	5″	× 6″

1951

OIL

66. Birds Like Cherries	16″	× 21″
67. Bubbles Don't Like Cats	8″	× 10″

WATERCOLOR

68. Petunias	10″	× 14″
69. Lily	5¼″	× 5¾″

1952

OIL

70. Berries and Grapes	8″	× 10″
71. Exhibit Flowers	16″	× 21″

WATERCOLOR

72. Doe Run Bridge	4″	× 6″
73. Camelia	8″	× 10″
74. Camelias	9″	× 11″
75. Wedding Cake House	8″	× 10″
76. Christ's Baptism	11″	× 14″

PENCILED DRAWING

77. Exhibit Flowers	7¼″ × 8″

1953

OIL

78. Petunias	14″	× 18″
79. Fall Flowers	10″	× 13″
80. Bubbles Don't Like Cats	8″	× 10″
81. Light Red Rose	8″	× 10″
82. Maple Tree	4½″	× 6½″

WATERCOLOR

83. William O. Jones Homestead	11"	× 14"
84. Gloxinias	9"	× 11"
85. Beautiful Flowers	9"	× 12"
86. Roses	4"	× 6"
87. Gloxinias from Snow Shoe	8"	× 12"

1954

OIL

88. Daffodils	9"	× 12"
89. It's a Buck	14"	× 18"
90. Ercildoun Hall	12"	× 16"
91. Daisies	4"	× 6"
92. Strawberries	4"	× 6"
93. Bubbles	4"	× 6"
94. Porgie	2"	× 4"
95. Apples	6"	× 4"

WATERCOLOR

96. Maple Tree	16"	× 20"
97. Home of Peter Filkosky	15"	× 20"
98. Autumn	4"	× 6"

1955

OIL

99. Blacksmith Shop	14"	× 18"
100. Mums	14"	× 18"
101. Bike Wagon	14"	× 18"
102. Sale Day	20"	× 30"

Her Creations

103.	Daisies	10″	× 8″
104.	Daffodils	9″	× 12″
105.	Rose of 1892	9″	× 12″
106.	Bed of Daffodils	4″	× 6″
107.	Zenia	4″	× 6″
108.	Deer	4″	× 6″
109.	Daffodils	9″	× 13″
110.	Scene from Hospital Window	4″	× 6″
111.	Snow in April	4″	× 6″
112.	Porgie	4″	× 6″
113.	Grapes	4″	× 6″
114.	Cedar Trees	4″	× 6″
115.	Snow Storm	4″	× 6″
116.	Horseback Ride	4″	× 6″
117.	Coasting	4″	× 6″
118.	The Horse	4″	× 6″
119.	Doe Run Bridge	4″	× 6″
120.	Yellow Rose	4″	× 6″
121.	Milking Time	4″	× 6″
122.	Mums	5¼″	× 5¾″

PENCILED DRAWING

123.	Reproduction of Bird on Nest	9″	× 11¾″

1956

OIL

124.	Phlox	12″	× 16″
125.	Zenia	12″	× 16″
126.	White Mums	14″	× 18″
127.	Mums	14″	× 18″
128.	A Light Snow	9″	× 6″
129.	A Light Snow #2	9″	× 6″

WATERCOLOR

130. AFTER THE STORM—CHILDREN COASTING	10″	× 14″
131. ROSE	9″	× 12″
132. OUR TWINS' BIRTHPLACE, 1895	10″	× 14″
133. JOHN F. BANKS RESIDENCE	14″	× 18″
134. MY MOCK ORANGE BUSH	10″	× 14″
135. ROSE IN BLOOM	9″	× 12″
136. AFTER THE SALE	4″	× 6″
137. DAFFODIL	4″	× 6″

1957

OIL

138. THE TEN VIRGINS	12″	× 16″
139. ROE BOATING (sic)	14″	× 16″
140. BIRTHDAY FLOWERS	16″	× 20″

WATERCOLOR

141. DAISIES	9″	× 12″
142. DRAWING OF 1892	9″	× 12″
143. QUINTS	9″	× 12″
144. MORNING GLORY	10″	× 12″
145. BUBBLES WANTS KITTY TO COME DOWN	4″	× 6″
146. HOSPITAL FLOWERS	4″	× 6″
147. ROSES	4″	× 6″
148. CARNATION	4″	× 6″

1958

OIL

149. POINSETTIA	8″	× 10″

WATERCOLOR

150. HORSEBACK RIDERS	8″	× 10″
151. OUR RIDING	8″	× 10″

PENCILED DRAWING

152. BIRD ON NEST (drawn in 1886)	9″ × 12″
153. ROE BOATING (sic) (drawn in 1892)	8½″ × 10½″
154. ROSES (drawn in 1892)	8½″ × 10½″
155. LANDSCAPE SCENE (drawn in 1892)	8½″ × 10½″
156. FISHING (drawn in 1892)	8½″ × 10½″
157. HOUSE BY SIDE OF ROAD (drawn in 1891)	8½″ × 10½″
158. LANDSCAPE (drawn in 1892)	8½″ × 10½″
159. BIRD (drawn Jan. 20, 1892)	8½″ × 10½″
160. MOTHER/DAUGHTER (drawn in 1892)	8½″ × 10½″
161. PRACTICE (1892)	7¼″ × 9¾″

9

Commendations and Recognitions

The development of Mom's latent talent was timely, though late in relation to her calendar years. It brought joy, excitement, opportunity, and fulfillment involving new experiences, new friends, constructive use of leisure, and financial rewards at a period in life when most needed.

Invitations to exhibit her work or participate in art shows sponsored by clubs, galleries, and schools increased as news of her achievements spread.

Although her age created added interest, her work was judged on its merits, evaluated by a jury irrespective of age.

Below are highlights from some of the commendations and/or recognition she received:

December 29, 1949. The *Coatesville Record*, a local newspaper, had this to say after her participation in the annual fall show of the Chester County Art Association at Anderson Hall, State Teachers College:

> Her work is reminiscent of the paintings of Grandma Moses, who recently won fame with her "primitives." In both the observer sees the product of great natural talent, both unimproved

and unspoiled by training. . . . Mrs. Jones' pictures exhibit a freshness and innocence and a free imagination, which make many of them charming and some of them irresistible.

November 18, 1951. From an evaluation by the Committee on Exhibitions at Lincoln University in reference to her first one-man exhibition of paintings:

Although Mrs. Jones may properly be termed a primitive, that does not mean that her expression is without parallel in the traditions of art. In many ways her work recalls that of Henri Rousseau and Horace Pippin. Although she may not attain to the stature of Pippin or Rousseau in her expression, her works are creative and are fully deserving of our consideration and respect.

March 4, 1952. From an article in the *Philadelphia Tribune*:

GRANDMOTHER EXHIBITS ART WORK IN CURRENT PYRAMID SHOW—AGE WITH A NEW HOBBY. . . . Despite her seventy-seven years, Mrs. Ida E. Jones finds the world of art fascinating and rewarding. . . . She is the oldest of the artists whose works are on display in the current Pyramid Club Show. . . . Her oil painting of "Mums" won acclaim at the annual shows of Everyman's Gallery and the Pyramid, both of Philadelphia.

May 1953. From the *Daily Local News*, West Chester, Pennsylvania, relative to the annual Chester County Art Show:

Moonlight on the Lake [was] completed fifty years after it was begun. . . . A never ending flow of sketches, oils and watercolors has been created by Mrs. Ida E. Jones. . . . This flood has carried her to art exhibitions and placed her work before the eyes of art critics. By them she has been classified as "an exceptionally good primitive artist."

May 22, 1953. From the commendation on the Achievement Award of the Adams Community School, Coatesville, Pennsylvania:

When past seventy, your fertile mind turned to the creative arts as a medium for personality expression. So well have you pursued this hobby that you are becoming recognized nationally among art critics as a unique contributor in the field of human expression. Small wonder is it that at eighty your age is "like a frosty winter, frosty but kindly."

In recognition of your contribution to better living in Chester County, this citation is awarded.

June 1957. From the *Coatesville Record* (Mom was a patient in the Atkinson Memorial Hospital in Coatesville all the time):

ATKINSON HOSPITAL PATIENT SHOWS HOW "ATTITUDE" CAN HELP DOCTOR. . . . To forestall the drudgery of idleness as well as provide gifts for patients and friends, she converted her hospital bed into a workshop and has completed more than two dozen drawings in the past ten weeks. Her joy is in making others happy by giving specimens of her handiwork.

Her many interviews with reporters, radio personnel, artists, art critics, and magazine editors were interesting and revealing. These together with exhibition engagements and entertainment of customers in her home left few dull moments and made life a whirl of exciting ventures.

When asked by a news reporter about her reaction to her new career, she replied, "I really don't have enough hours in the day to do all the things that I'd like to do. It just seems that this was something I've always had to do as soon as I got around to it."

10

Ebb Tide

The pleasant dream of an early childhood interest that lingered throughout her life had matured into a reality, as flowers, birds, hills, valleys, and the rippling waters all seemed to burst with intense beauty, splendor, and new meaning.

Channeling her experiences into artistic expression enriched her life, gave her new purpose for living, and proved that one's active years need not end at retirement from regular duties or with widowhood or when the children leave home to pursue their own way of life.

Mom was now eighty-three. Her whole life was centered around her career in the world of art, with a few days now and then to visit the children and friends. Time out from the regular routine was good. She would then return to her cherished hobby with renewed zeal.

About this time, an old physical problem began to trouble her anew, making it necessary for her to spend some time with her daughter Blanche E. Johnson, of Ercildoun, rather than remain in her home alone. Her ailment also limited the production of new paintings and participation in the annual art shows of 1957 and 1958.

When her physical problems worsened in the spring of 1957 she required hospitalization. But this did not stop her. Though hospitalized, she still demonstrated her love of painting. Her hospital bed became her workshop and she completed small paintings of views from the hospital window, fruits, trees, and other subjects of interest. Upon her discharge from the hospital after a ten-week stay, she resumed her art work at home in a minor way.

January 1959 marked the beginning of a critical condition. She was admitted again to the Atkinson Memorial Hospital.

January 31, 1959, marked the end of a beautiful and full life.

Mr. Thomas J. Anderson, principal of Adams Community School, gave this final tribute:

> She left behind a radiance that shines beyond the sunset; the glory of a productive life; the realization that age does not end one's useful, constructive years, and the memory of a beautiful life shared and lived with others.

11

Posthumous Exhibits

FEBRUARY 22—MARCH 24, 1974
DELAWARE ART MUSEUM

Mom's work, along with three other Delaware Valley primitives—Henry Braunstein and Edward C. Kimmel from Wilmington, Delaware, and Horace Pippin of West Chester, Pennsylvania—was exhibited at the Delaware Art Museum, Wilmington, Delaware. The exhibition provided an opportunity for the public to take a look at primitive painting of artists with widely differing, highly individual styles and varying backgrounds, painting experience, and ability.

This first major museum exhibition of her work was organized by museum interns Cynthia Bell and Susan Strickler, with the cooperation of many collectors and museums throughout the area and the East.

The following paintings were displayed:

1. JONES HOME (1951, watercolor) Lent by Mr. and Mrs. Robert Wood, Swarthmore, Pennsylvania
2. A LOAD OF LIVESTALK (sic) (oil) Lent by Mrs. Walter P. Townsend

3. SPRINGTIME 1892 (1952, oil) Lent by Mrs. Walter P. Townsend
4. BEFORE FREEDOM (1954, gouache) Lent by Mrs. Walter P. Townsend
5. PINK MUMS (1956, oil) Lent by Mrs. Walter P. Townsend
6. DEER SEASON (1954, oil) Lent by Mrs. Walter P. Townsend
7. TUGBOAT, CAPE CHARLES, VIRGINIA (oil) Lent by Mr. and Mrs. Karl de Schweinitz
8. PASTURE SEASON (oil) Lent by Mrs. Walter P. Townsend
9. STRAWBERRIES AND GRAPES (watercolor) Lent by Mr. and Mrs. Karl de Schweinitz
10. WE TRAVELED THIS WAY IN 1892 (oil) Lent by Mrs. Walter P. Townsend
11. STRAWBERRIES AND GRAPES (watercolor) Lent by Mr. Peter Hallinger
12. OUR HOUSE CAT—OLD TOM (watercolor) Lent by Mrs. Walter P. Townsend
13. PARABLE OF THE TEN VIRGINS (oil) Lent by Mrs. Walter P. Townsend
14. CAMELIAS (oil) Lent by Mrs. Walter P. Townsend

MAY 10, 1976—ERCILDOUN BICENTENNIAL

When the village of Ercildoun held its Bicentennial celebration, Mom's paintings were among those of other residents of the community. The following paintings were exhibited:

1. MOCK ORANGE BUSH (1956, watercolor) Lent by Mrs. Ingrid Jones
2. ABOVE LANCASTER (1949, oil) Lent by Mrs. Ida J. Williams
3. VIRGINIA'S DOGWOOD (1945, oil) Lent by Mrs. Ida J. Williams
4. EXHIBIT FLOWERS (1952, oil) Lent by Mrs. Ida J. Williams
5. MOONLIGHT ON THE LAKE (1950, oil) Lent by Mrs. Ida J. Williams

Posthumous Exhibits

MARCH 12—MARCH 26, 1978
THE CHESTER COUNTY ART ASSOCIATION

The gallery at 100 North Bradford Avenue, West Chester, Pennsylvania, exhibited the nine paintings below. All the paintings were owned by Mrs. Walter P. Townsend.

1. A LOAD OF LIVESTALK (sic) (1951, oil)
2. SPRINGTIME IN 1892 (1952, oil)
3. PINK MUMS (1956, oil)
4. DEER SEASON (1954, oil)
5. PASTURE SEASON (1954, oil)
6. WE TRAVELED THIS WAY IN 1892 (1955, oil)
7. OUR HOUSE CAT, OLD TOM (1948, watercolor)
8. PARABLE OF THE TEN VIRGINS (1957, oil)
9. CAMELIAS (1952, oil)

12

Biographical Highlights

Ida Ella Ruth was born to Samuel and Louisa Ruth on February 4, 1874, in a small stone dwelling near the village of Chatham, Pennsylvania. She was the third daughter in a family of ten children (four sons and six daughters), namely, Robert Frederick, Bertha, Samuel, Mary Elizabeth, Ida Ella, George Edward, Leah Louisa, Sarah Amy, William Chester, and Retta Isabella.

Her father, a former slave, was among those who were freed by the Civil War. He came north to Massachusetts and joined the 54th Massachusetts Volunteers under Captain John McPherson.

After the war he left Massachusetts and went on his own to New Jersey, then to Fredericksburg, Virginia, where he met and married Louisa Pinn. They migrated to Pennsylvania, settling in Chatham where their family began to increase. A final move was made to the Ercildoun area where the last of the children were to be born.

Her formal schooling was limited due to the number of chores that needed to be carried out on the farm on which the family lived—cows to be milked then the milk carried to the old spring house for cooling, butter to be churned, eggs to be gathered and stored, garden crops to be planted and kept weeded, fruits, vegetables, and meats to be conserved for the long cold winter months.

Because of the excellent way that she handled her younger brothers and sisters, the child-care responsibilities fell to her while her mother was away, serving as a midwife to many in the community. As early as eight years of age, she was standing on a little stool in front of the old kitchen stove preparing cooked cereal and other simple dishes for the young family members.

When she reached her teen years, she helped to supplement the family income by doing housework for Mrs. Lucretia Haines who lived in the village of Ercildoun. It was here that her artistic ability was observed and encouraged.

In 1887, a young apprentice blacksmith began work with William Harvey, owner of the Ercildoun Blacksmith Shop, for whom he served three years. The young apprentice, William Oscar Jones, attended services at the local Church of Christ, where he met Mom and the rest of her family. A quiet, serious romance bloomed, until, upon completion of his training, he asked for her hand in marriage.

The entire Ruth family busied themselves for weeks getting the home, food and delicacies, gifts, and wedding attire just right for the occasion. They were married on December 28, 1893.

A new way of life began, filled with numerous experiences, events, and additions to the family.

The two of them became ardent workers for the church, where Mom's beautiful soprano voice led to the responsibility of song leader for the congregation. Pop's leadership abilities and ministerial qualities earned for him the responsibility of an Elder of the congregation. The two made an inspirational team for the youth to emulate—one preaching the gospel and the other singing it, both living it in word and deed.

Church, family, and community commitments filled every moment, leaving little time for anything else. The family continued to grow until there were Joseph Haines, Anna and Umphert (twins lost in infancy), Laura Louise, Blanche Ellen, Samuel Ruth, William Alfred, Harold Valentine, Ida Eliza Katherine, Charles Francis, Owen Leon, and Lucy May.

From time to time physical problems would plague Mom, until in the fall of 1945 the doctor ordered her to curtail her activities and household chores; it was then that she returned to painting.

On April 6, 1947, she was widowed, after fifty-three years of an endearing and rewarding marriage.

In 1950, Dr. Horace Bond, president of Lincoln University, on a chance visit, discovered her. He set the wheels in motion for her first one-man exhibition of paintings. From then on, her paintings attracted attention wherever she exhibited them.

Her first exhibit was at the Chester County Art Association's Annual Spring Show in 1950. She continued to participate in their exhibitions throughout her career.

Other places where her paintings have been exhibited are the Philadelphia Art Alliance—Everyman's Gallery, The Pyramid Club, Ellen Donovan Gallery in the Philadelphia area; the YWCA of Coatesville, sponsored by the Soroptomist Club; the Adams Community School, Coatesville; Speakman's Bookstore, Coatesville; Delaware Art Museum, Wilmington Delaware; and the Chester County Art Gallery, West Chester, Pennsylvania.

Mrs. Walter P. Townsend, a great admirer of her work, introduced her to many persons interested in the field of art. She also used her own time to plan and sponsor a one-man exhibition of her paintings in her home. She also took her on rides through the country in search of interesting subjects for her paintings and assisted her in getting to the art shows in the Philadelphia area.

Mom was very grateful for her many kind deeds and for making it possible for much of the recognition she received.

Mr. Allan Wolf, a noted art collector from New York City who had heard of Mom, visited her at home and purchased a number of her paintings. He sponsored an exhibition of her work in New York.

From 1945 to 1958 Mom took advantage of every opportunity for artistic expression through her creative talent. She saw beauty everywhere—an ordinary flower in bloom, a simple bowl of strawberries, a bird on the wing, children at play, hills and valleys.

She continued to be active until a critical illness necessitated her return to the hospital where a beautiful and great life ended on January 31, 1959.

Each year of her life was filled with joy, challenges, achievement, contentment, and happiness. The calendar years set no barriers. She proved that life is what we make it.

Charlotte C. Kinney must have had a person like her in mind when she wrote the following poem:

MOMENTS

> We live in moments—shining moments only,
> That prick the drab fabric of our existence
> As stars pierce the night.
> Moments of beauty and high adventure;
> Moments when we glimpse life's meaning—
> An endless quest, a making of new goals,
> Never an arriving.
> Moments of love and understanding,
> Courage, honor, dedication,
> Kindness and generosity.
> Moments when we can shout for the joys of mere living.
> Moments of satisfaction in life's common experiences—
> In the family, in friendship, in work,
> In the enjoyment of art and the out-of-doors;
> Thank God for our radiant moments!

May the life of this noble character—my Mom—serve as an inspiration to both young and old alike.